D1758090

WAT

Please renew or return items by the date shown on your receipt

www.hertfordshire.gov.uk/libraries

Renewals and enquiries: 0300 123 4049

Textphone for hearing or 0300 123 4041
speech impaired users:

L32 11.16

Hertfordshire

526 077 55 7

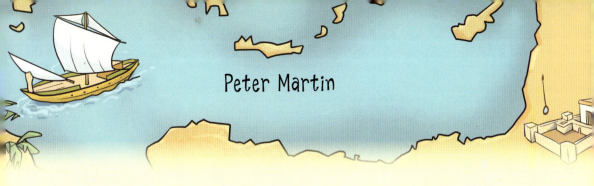

Peter Martin

A TIME-TRAVEL GUIDE TO
THE LAND OF
JESUS

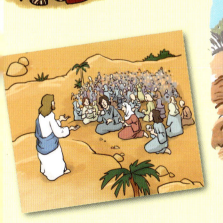

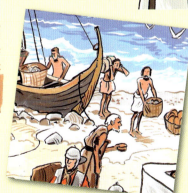

LION
CHILDREN'S

Text by Peter Martin
Illustrations copyright © 2017 Dave Smith and
Emmanuel Cerisier
This edition copyright © 2017 Lion Hudson

Published by Lion Children's Books
an imprint of
Lion Hudson plc
Wilkinson House, Jordan Hill Road,
Oxford OX2 8DR, England
www.lionhudson.com/lionchildrens

ISBN 978 0 7459 6589 5

First edition 2017

A catalogue record for this book is available from the
British Library

Printed and bound in China, January 2017, LH06

Text acknowledgments
Many thanks to Victoria Tebbs for all her assistance with
this book.

Bible extracts are taken or adapted from the Good
News Bible © 1994 published by the Bible Societies/
HarperCollins Publishers Ltd UK, Good News Bible©
American Bible Society 1966, 1971, 1976, 1992. Used
with permission.

Image acknowledgments
David Alexander: 26t, 35t, 36, 49t

David Townsend: 11t, 33t, 38b

istock: 5t/Rostislav Ageev, 12t/Boris Katsman, 15c/Asafta
51t/andegro4ka

John Williams: 13bl, 27br

Lion Hudson: 40t, 45t, 50t, 50b, 56t

Lois Rock: 29t

Peter Dennis: 11b, 34b

Rex Nicholls: 6b, 13tr, 13br, 24–25, 41t

Shutterstock: 52t/Radko Fabian

Zev Radovan, Bible Land Pictures: 29br, 32c, 59tr

Contents

Putting Galilee on the Map

On the eastern shore of the Mediterranean Sea, north of the city of Jerusalem, and just a short distance inland, lies the Jewish region of Galilee.

The year is AD 50 and more and more tourists are visiting this little-known area. The reason it's becoming so popular is down to a local preacher who lived here: Jesus of Nazareth.

LET'S GO TO GALILEE!

Ben

Rachel

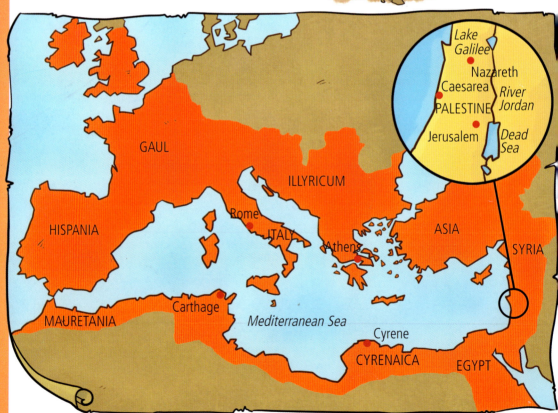

The extent of the Roman empire in the 1st century AD

Lake Galilee is a must-see destination for visitors to the region

Jesus was born in the town of Bethlehem, near Jerusalem, but spent much of his boyhood in Nazareth. Later he made his home in the town of Capernaum, by the shores of Lake Galilee. But he was constantly moving from place to place, talking to people and healing those who were ill.

Since Jesus' death, the number of people claiming to be his followers has increased dramatically. Many say he performed miracles, and even claim he was the Son of God, who was taken up into heaven. They have numerous stories to tell about what he did and said, and take his teaching very seriously.

Now hundreds of others are interested in finding out about Jesus and in seeing the places where he lived and taught.

This book will help you take a tour: through Galilee and beyond. Now is a good time to visit, while Galilee is still relatively unspoiled. You will discover beautiful scenery and plenty of interesting local culture. Look out for our tourist tips, must-see recommendations, and best buys along the way!

TOURIST TIP

Make sure you pack some comfortable walking sandals – there will be lots of places to see and things to do!

Useful Information

Here is some useful information for all 1st-century travellers to Galilee and the surrounding area.

POLITICAL SITUATION

The land you are visiting is inhabited mainly by Jewish people. It is also part of the Roman empire. Roman troops make sure that Roman laws are obeyed and taxes are paid. However, they are unlikely to pick on tourists unless you are unruly.

The beautiful Galilean countryside is, surprisingly, not as calm as it may seem. Skirmishes between Roman troops and Jewish freedom fighters can break out anywhere. So be prepared to move on.

CURRENCY

The Jewish people have their own currency but it is hard to get hold of in advance. Roman coins, such as *denarii*, are available everywhere in the empire, and provincial coins can be obtained at ports and in major towns.

Some Jewish traders will reject Roman coins because they don't like Roman rule.

Mediterranean Sea

Mount Hermon

Caesarea Philippi

GALILEE
Capernaum
Cana
Bethsaida
Lake Galilee
Nazareth
Gadara
Caesarea
Bethany
Sychar
R. Jordan
SAMARIA
Jericho
Jerusalem
Bethany
Bethlehem
JUDEA
Dead Sea

Region of Galilee

Popular places to visit in Galilee and further afield

Various different types of coins are used across the region

LANGUAGE

The local Jewish population speak Aramaic although their written language is Hebrew. Latin is the official language of the empire. Most people can get by in Greek.

HEALTH

There is very little in the way of health care, so take care of yourself and pack a first-aid kit. Make sure the food you eat is properly cooked and prepared. Water from village wells is usually quite good.

GETTING AROUND

There are many interesting places to visit in and around Galilee. To make the most of your time, consider hiring a donkey for short journeys. But beware – they can be very stubborn!

LAKE GALILEE IS THAT WAY!

IDENTITY CARD

If you have proof of being a Roman citizen, take that with you, as you will probably get better treatment from any officials you come across. However, it's unlikely you will be asked to show any identification papers on your travels.

Getting There

A major Roman road runs through Galilee, providing an easy route for overland travellers from Syria and Asia in the north, and from Egypt in the south.

If you are journeying by sea, the port of Caesarea on Palestine's west coast has a massive harbour built by King Herod the Great. From here it is a short overland trip to Galilee.

WHERE DO YOU WANT TO GO FIRST, RACHEL?

Tanais

Olbia

GAUL

Genoa

Narbo

ILLYRICUM

Black Sea

Tarraco

Rome

Thessalonica

Byzantium

Ostia

ITALY

ASIA

Ephesus

Antioch

Palermo

Rhegium

SYRIA

Carthage

Corinth

Caesarea

Mediterranean Sea

Jerusalem

Cyrene

Alexandria

CYRENAICA

EGYPT

—— main Roman road

HIPPODROME
CHARIOT RACE
NEXT SATURDAY AT 2 P.M.
WITH GUEST APPEARANCE
BY GOLDEN BOY
FLAVIUS

MUST SEE!

Caesarea

If you pass through Caesarea, you may want to spend a day or so exploring the sights before travelling on to Galilee. There is a superb amphitheatre and an impressive aqueduct. Chariot races are held at the hippodrome, which can hold up to 20,000 spectators!

Who Was Jesus?

Jesus was born in about 5 BC and died when he was thirty-two or thirty-three. He grew up in Nazareth in Galilee with his mother Mary and her husband Joseph. From Joseph he learned the carpentry trade.

Jesus became a preacher when he was around thirty and gathered a large following. Many people who saw him say that he could work miracles and that he healed people just by touching them.

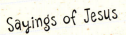

Sayings of Jesus

"Treat others as you want to be treated."

"Love one another."

"Forgive others the wrongs they do to you, and God will forgive your wrongdoing."

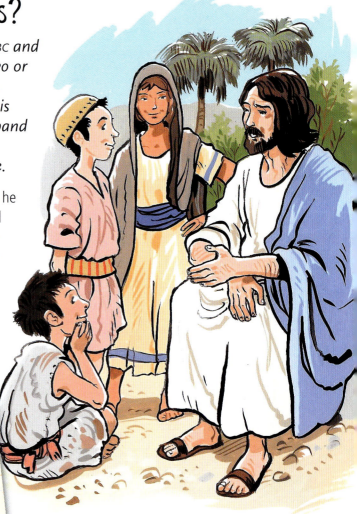

Jesus preached about God and the way God wants people to live

MESSIAH

The followers of Jesus claim that he was the Son of God and the messiah – a word that means "chosen king".

Long ago, the Jews were an independent nation. Their greatest king – David, who was a shepherd boy living near Bethlehem – remains a hero. Nowadays, the lands around the Mediterranean Sea, including Galilee, are part of the Roman empire. The dream of the Jewish people is that one day a heroic king like David – a messiah – will come and set them free from Roman rule.

THE KINGDOM OF GOD

Jesus' followers say Jesus was the messiah, but not the kind of heroic king the Jews were expecting. Instead of overthrowing those who were in charge, Jesus invited everyone to be part of the "kingdom of God" – a kind of virtual kingdom of people who would live as God's friends.

Before Jesus was crucified he wore a crown of thorns

CRUCIFIXION

After three years as a preacher Jesus was hated by the religious leaders. They thought he did not show proper respect for Jewish traditions. However, they didn't have the authority to have him put to death. They told the Roman governor, Pontius Pilate, that Jesus was a rebel who wanted to be "king of the Jews". Pilate handed Jesus over to be crucified.

RESURRECTION

Three days later, Jesus' body vanished from his tomb. His close friends claim he was alive again and appeared to them several times before being taken up to heaven.

JESUS' FOLLOWERS

Jesus' followers today are known for taking care of one another. They believe they are already part of God's kingdom and will live for ever in God's heaven.

David was just a shepherd boy but became a king and hero

Nazareth

Many visitors to Galilee head for Nazareth, among the hills. This is the town where Jesus grew up. Its streets and houses are much the same as they would have been in his day.

Gentle hills surround the town of Nazareth

Synagogue

Schoolroom

Potter's workshop

Carpenter's workshop

CARPENTER'S WORKSHOP

Jesus grew up as the son of Joseph the carpenter, learning how to work with wood and stone. Other family members are still in the same trade, making farm equipment – wheels, carts, ox yokes, threshing sleds, and the like.

MUST SEE!

SCHOOLROOM

Next to the synagogue is a room where the local teacher, the rabbi, runs a school for boys. It is almost certainly the very same place Jesus would have learned to read and write.

One piece of writing Jesus probably learned is the *shema*, which is from Hebrew scriptures. It means this: "Hear, O Israel, the Lord is our God, the Lord alone."

BEST BUY

These tie-on leather sandals, of the kind that Jesus wore, are still very popular. You'll be sure to find a cheap pair from one of the market stalls.

Jesus would have learned to write Hebrew using a wax writing tablet and a pointed wooden stylus

SYNAGOGUE

You can still see the synagogue where Jesus read aloud. It is laid out in the traditional way, with the scrolls in a cupboard at the back and a lectern where Jesus may have stood to read.

The *menorah* is a seven-branched lampstand which serves as a reminder of the menorah Moses made for the tabernacle and which for many is a symbol of the Jewish faith.

Menorah

JESUS FACT FILE

Stories of Jesus' life are being carefully collected by his followers. One of the accounts tells of a dark episode in Nazareth's recent past.

Murder most failed

One day, when Jesus was just starting out as a preacher, he was invited to read aloud in the synagogue. He was handed the scroll of the prophet Isaiah.

"The Spirit of the Lord is upon me," he read, "because he has chosen me to bring good news to the poor… and announce that the time has come when the Lord will save his people."

Jesus handed the scroll back and turned to face the people. They were expecting that, as a preacher, he would explain the meaning.

"Today," said Jesus, "this passage has come true."

In other words, he was saying he was God's chosen one. The people were furious! No way was their local carpenter a prophet of God.

Things got ugly. The men gathered around Jesus and marched him off to teach him a lesson. Rumour has it that they tried to push him over a nearby cliff. No one is sure where this was, but some believe it was at the Mount of Precipitation, which is about two kilometres from Nazareth.

Somehow Jesus managed to slip away through the crowds, but from then on he did not feel welcome in his hometown.

The Mount of Precipitation, near Nazareth

DO YOU FANCY GOING UP THE MOUNT OF PRECIPITATION? OR SHALL WE GO SHOPPING INSTEAD?

TOURIST TIP

If you fancy a day trip to the mountains, just be careful – no mountain rescue services exist. Do not attempt to scramble up the cliffs. All ascents are at your own risk.

Capernaum

Capernaum is a popular tourist destination in Galilee. This bustling fishing village became Jesus' new home after he left Nazareth.

He was welcomed by one of the local fishermen, Simon. Jesus gave him the nickname Peter, which means "rock".

Capernaum is where Jesus is said to have healed many sick and disabled people, including Simon Peter's mother-in-law.

Synagogue

Lots of the fish that are caught are dried and salted to preserve them.

The mild climate in Galilee enables people to spend much of their time outside, either in courtyards or on rooftops.

 TOURIST TIP

Beware of rogues at places where Jesus is said to have healed people. People know that Jesus' followers want to help the sick and disabled, and tricksters pretend to be suffering. But all they want is for you to give them some money!

 JESUS FACT FILE

Healing the sick

Jesus took Simon Peter's mother-in-law by the hand and lifted her up, and her fever immediately left her.

Capernaum's Waterfront

Capernaum is a fishing town and you will see many boats tied up along the stone jetties. Fresh fish will be on sale from early morning, and locally grown herbs and vegetables are also widely available.

FISHING

You will have to get up very early if you want to see fishermen actually out in their boats. There are various different types of nets used for fishing: dragnets, cast nets, and trammel nets.

Trammel nets – these are nets that have two large mesh walls with a finer mesh in between, and which are pulled around into a circle to trap the fish.

MUST SEE!

Trammel net fishing

Cast nets – these are circular nets measuring around six metres in diameter and are thrown from a boat.

Dragnets – these can be over thirty metres long and several metres high. They are dropped over the side of the boat, with the bottom end weighted down with sinkers. Then one team of fishermen on the shore pull the net in using ropes.

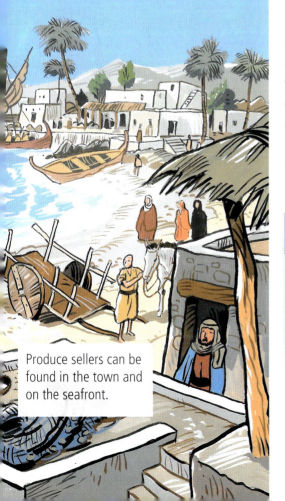

Produce sellers can be found in the town and on the seafront.

 JESUS FACT FILE

Fishing for people

Jesus called four fishermen – Simon Peter, Andrew, James, and John – to be his first followers, or disciples. He told them to leave their nets and come to fish for people – gathering them into friendship with God, "God's kingdom". Simon Peter and Andrew were probably using a cast net when they met Jesus for the first time.

EATING OUT

Locals are making the most of the tourist trade. Some prepare food you can take and eat for lunch, such as bread stuffed with cooked fish and herbs.

Others are offering visitors a home-cooked dinner on their rooftops.

BEST BUY

Fish is widely available and a speciality of the region. The main kinds of fish that are caught in Lake Galilee are musht (also called tilapia), sardines, and barbels.

MUSHT – BUY NOW!

Jesus at Lake Galilee

Jesus spent much of his time as a preacher visiting the towns and villages around Lake Galilee. It is here that he is believed to have performed many of his miracles. These places have become popular tourist spots, but remember that people will make different claims about what happened where.

• Magdala is famous as the home town of Mary Magdalene, who first saw the risen Jesus.

• Tiberias is still being developed. It is hoped tourists will come to enjoy the hot springs. It's possible that when Jesus was a carpenter, he worked on the building sites here.

• Followers of Jesus say that he and his friends were once caught in a storm on Lake Galilee and that Jesus stilled the wind and waves with just a word.

• In the territory of Gadara Jesus healed two men who were possessed by demons. Jesus ordered the demons to go into a herd of pigs, which then stampeded off a cliff into the lake.

Magdala

Tiberias

Gadara

• Between Capernaum and Bethsaida is the place where Jesus is said to have appeared to seven of his disciples after his death... They saw someone grilling fish on the shore. It was Jesus. There, he asked Simon Peter to be in charge of carrying on his work.

TOURIST TIP

Boats are a convenient way to travel. Some will take tourists to the places linked to Jesus. A round-the-lake trip is best spread over two days.

Make sure you don't take a boat when the weather is stormy – the hills around Lake Galilee funnel the wind, and conditions can soon become treacherous.

Capernaum

Bethsaida

Lake Galilee

• Bethsaida is said to be where Jesus and his disciples went by boat to be alone. But the crowds went around the shore on foot to find them. Jesus had pity on them and healed many who were ill. Then, miraculously, Jesus fed all 5,000 of them by sharing out just five loaves and two fish.

Hiking from Nazareth to Capernaum

One great way to enjoy rural Galilee is to walk the hillside trails from Nazareth to Capernaum – just as Jesus did. No one knows the exact path Jesus took. However, followers of Jesus have begun treading one route that takes in some key places in Jesus' life, and you can do this comfortably over three days.

Day One: Nazareth to Cana

Cana is a rural village with vineyards on the south-facing hillsides nearby.

 JESUS FACT FILE

The wedding at Cana

The story goes that Jesus and his mother Mary were invited to a wedding in Cana. The guests were having a great party, but the wine was running out. Jesus told the servants to fill some jars with water and then draw some out to put in pitchers. By a miracle, the water had become wine.

WEDDING TRADITIONS

A wedding is a big community event. If you happen to be staying in Cana or any other small community it is very likely that you will be invited to join in the party.

The bride and groom will sit under a canopy.

Don't have a partner to dance with? Just grab a tambourine and dance in your own style. You won't be alone for long.

once you're invited in, help yourself to food and drink.

SLEEPING OUT

Sleeping out under the stars is quite common in Galilee. It is a good idea to ask locals for their advice. They will be able to suggest places where you are unlikely to be bothered – either by people or animals. An empty shed is great for this.

You don't want to wake up to find a goat eating your blanket!

Vineyard Tour Around Cana

Highly recommended for any visitor is a tour of a local wine press, and one of the several vineyards around Cana. A guide will show you the equipment used for extracting the juice from the grapes and will explain the processes involved in making wine. Many grape farmers will use the same press, as it's too expensive to have their own. Some wine presses use a method of stacking baskets of grapes on top of one another, while others have a pit in which workers tread the grapes.

MUST SEE!

Labourers scare off birds from a watchtower.

Stone walls keep out wild animals which might damage the vines.

Grapevines

Earthenware jars are filled from this large vat of grape juice.

TOURIST TIP

Vineyard owners will be eager to sell you wine to take away, either in an amphora or a wineskin. If it's new wine, check that it is being sold in a new wineskin. The fermenting process in new wine can burst old wineskins that have lost their stretchiness.

A heavy flat weight is placed on top of the baskets.

Baskets filled with grapes are stacked on top of one another and the grape juice filters through.

Day Two: Over the Hills

The second day of your trek from Nazareth to Capernaum will be very rural.

Here is a guide to some of the kinds of farming activities you might see.

This is known as the Gezer calendar and dates back to the time of King David's son Solomon. It is a rhyme to remind farmers what time of year to plant and harvest.

Spring

Cutting flax

Summer

Threshing

Winnowing

Autumn

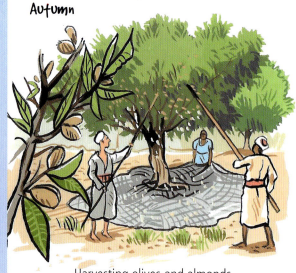

Harvesting olives and almonds

Winter

Sowing seeds

JESUS FACT FILE

The parable of the sower

In his preaching Jesus often used situations from farming to help his listeners understand what he was saying. For example, he talked about people who hear his teaching.

• Those who forget it immediately are like seed flung on the path, which is eaten by birds.

• Those who hear but then forget are like seed on thin, rocky soil. The plants grow but soon wither in the sun.

• Those who try to obey the teaching but whose everyday worries get in the way are like seeds among thorn bushes. They cannot grow properly.

• Those who hear and change their lives for the good are like seed grown on good soil, bearing a good harvest. These are the people who are part of God's kingdom.

TOURIST TIP

You can easily lose your way in the remote countryside, so you may wish to hire a guide to help you. But just remember that you'll probably be given a young local lad who may not want to wait for stragglers!

Can you keep up?

BEST BUY

Flax is widely grown for linen. Some nice cloths for drying dishes make a lovely gift to take back home.

MOTHER WILL LOVE SOME LINEN TEA TOWELS!

A Remote Night

After the second day of hiking you will be in remote countryside, and you will need to think carefully about where you are going to sleep.

OPTION ONE

Find a farm or a hamlet where you can spend the night. Your hosts will provide food and water, but don't bank on getting a roof over your head – if space is tight, you may end up sleeping on the roof!

TOURIST TIP

Have plenty of coins to pay what you agree as the price. Rural folk are mainly self-sufficient and they may not have change.

OPTION TWO

Try to find some friendly shepherds who will let you stay with them. Shepherds always stay out on the hills in order to look after their flocks and protect them from wild animals and robbers. At night the sheep are kept in a sheepfold, made of stone walls, and the shepherds make their camp just by the gate. This is where you will also be able to sleep. But remember to wrap up well as it can get very cold, even after a warm day.

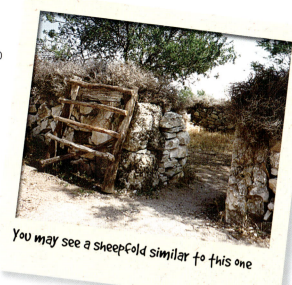

You may see a sheepfold similar to this one

Look out for...

lions

bears

jackals

JESUS FACT FILE

The good shepherd

Jesus described himself as "the good shepherd". He meant that, just as a shepherd protects his sheep and leads them to good pasture, so he would do all he could to look after his followers and lead them to happiness and to God. He said, "I have come in order that you may have life – life in all its fullness."

A shepherd among his flock

Day Three: Where Jesus Taught

The final day of your hike will bring you through the countryside near Capernaum to a hill where Jesus is said to have addressed huge crowds.

Jesus' message was about how people should live their lives, and how they could become friends of God and part of God's kingdom.

JESUS FACT FILE

The Sermon on the Mount

Jesus said:

"Do not worry about the food and drink you need, or about clothes… Your Father in heaven takes care of the birds… and clothes the wild grasses. Won't he be all the more sure to clothe you? Instead, be concerned about the kingdom of God."

"Love your enemies."

"Do not judge others, so that God will not judge you."

And he spoke about what makes people truly happy:

"Happy are those who are merciful to others; God will be merciful to them!

"Happy are the pure in heart; they will see God!

"Happy are those who work for peace; God will call them his children!"

TOURIST TIP

From this spot you can be back at Capernaum in around an hour. After your long hike, it's worth paying a bit extra for a nice place to stay.

ooh, lovely!

Ask a servant to bring a bowl of water so that you can wash your feet – they will be very dusty!

Caesarea Philippi and Mount Hermon

The town of Caesarea Philippi is situated around thirty kilometres north of Lake Galilee. Here a stream flows out of a cliff before joining the River Jordan.

Carved into the rock are niches for shrines to the Greek god Pan. Half human and half goat, Pan is revered by some as the god of sheep, wild places, and music.

JESUS FACT FILE

The messiah

In Caesarea Philippi Jesus is said to have asked his disciples who people thought he was. Simon Peter replied, "You are the messiah, the Christ, the Son of the living God."

Niches in the rock at Caesarea Philippi, where some people worshipped the Greek god Pan

Near the shrines traders will try to sell you "pan pipes"

PLEASE STOP IT, BEN!

Beyond Caesarea Philippi lies the region of Mount Hermon. It is a huge highland area dotted with peaks that are, in fact, old volcanoes. The highest, Mount Hermon, is some 2,800 metres above sea level.

Look out for...

wild flowers in spring

eagles and other birds of prey

wild goats

 JESUS FACT FILE

The transfiguration

Jesus is said to have taken three of his disciples – Simon Peter, James, and John – up a mountain, which many believe was Mount Hermon. Once they were alone Jesus was "transfigured" – his face started shining like the sun and his clothes became a dazzling white. Two prophets of olden times, Moses and Elijah, also appeared. Seeing this made the disciples even surer that Jesus was not an ordinary person.

Samaria

If you wish to travel from Galilee to tourist hotspots in Judea, such as Jerusalem and Bethlehem, the most convenient route is to pass through the region of Samaria.

This is not territory where Jewish people live: Jews and Samaritans have been hostile towards one another for hundreds of years owing to disagreements about traditions of worship. Many Jews are willing to make a long detour to reach cities in the south, so they don't have to go through Samaria.

⭐ JESUS FACT FILE

Stories of Jesus show that, even though he was a Jew, he did not look down on Samaritans.

The woman at the well

One day Jesus was on his way back to Galilee from Judea and was travelling through Samaria. He came to a place named Sychar. Tired out, he sat down at a well there. A Samaritan woman approached, and Jesus asked her to draw some water. It was very unusual for Jews to speak to Samaritans. But Jesus began talking to her about God. During their conversation he told her that the place of worship – whether the Temple in Jerusalem for the Jews, or a special mountain for the Samaritans – was less important than worshipping God with a true heart and true faith.

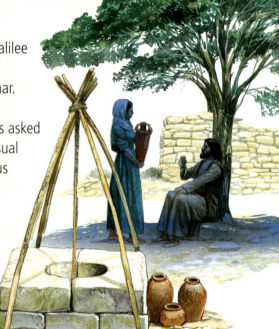

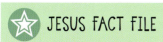

JESUS FACT FILE

The good Samaritan

Another time, Jesus told a Jewish teacher of the Law, "Love your neighbour as you love yourself." The teacher didn't really understand and asked, "Who is my neighbour?" So Jesus told him a story about a man who was mugged on a lonely road leading to Jerusalem. A priest and a Temple worker walked past but did nothing to help. Then a Samaritan came by. He stopped, tended to the man, and paid an innkeeper to look after him. This story became known as the parable of the "Good Samaritan".

on a remote road such as this, there aren't many passers-by

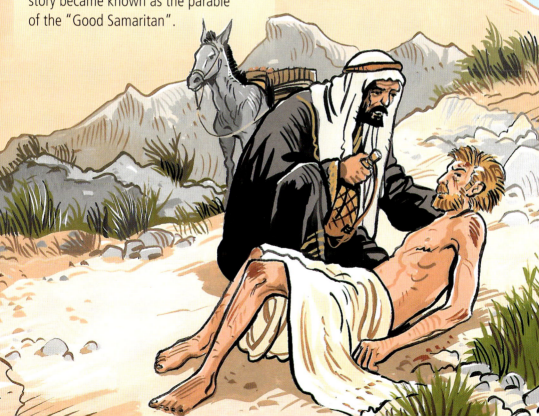

Bethany on the River Jordan

The distance from the source of the River Jordan to the point where the river empties into the Dead Sea is over 200 kilometres. Yet the river is far longer than that, owing to its winding course. It's too far for most tourists to travel the length of it on foot, but one popular destination is the village of Bethany. It was here that Jesus is said to have been baptized by his cousin John.

⭐ JESUS FACT FILE

John the Baptist

At the time that Jesus began preaching, John the Baptist was journeying throughout the land near the River Jordan, telling people to change their ways. He said if they did this, God would forgive their sins. Many crowds came to him to be baptized in the river. John kept telling them about someone important who was going to come. "I am not good enough even to untie his sandals," he said.

Jesus' baptism

The story goes that Jesus travelled to a place named Bethany to be baptized by John. At first, John hesitated. He said, "I ought to be baptized by you!" But Jesus

TOURIST TIP

It can be tempting to swim in the river, but beware:
* The water may be deeper and the current faster than it looks, especially after rain.
* Think about what you are going to wear. Swimming with no clothes on is frowned upon.

gently urged him to do things in the way God wanted, and so he agreed. People believe that, when Jesus had been baptized, the Spirit of God in the form of a dove flew down. And a voice said, "This is my own dear Son, with whom I am pleased."

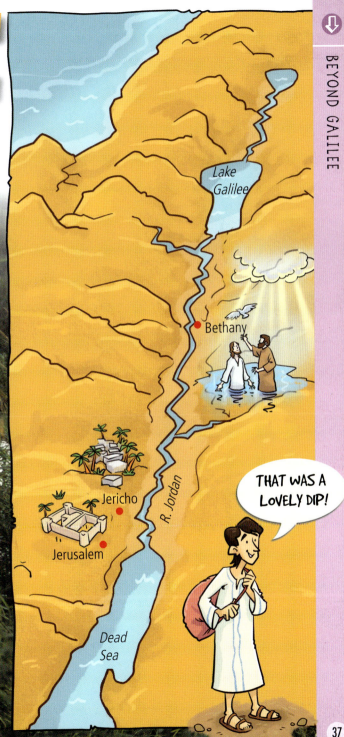

Lake Galilee

Bethany

Jericho

R. Jordan

Jerusalem

Dead Sea

THAT WAS A LOVELY DIP!

37

Jericho

Further south and a little to the west of the River Jordan lies the city of Jericho. One of the oldest cities in the world, it is well worth a visit.

Situated at a low altitude, the weather can be very warm; however the springs ensure that the soil is well watered and the whole area surrounding the city is very fertile. Dates are a particular speciality.

Throughout the streets of Jericho you will find areas that are pleasantly shaded by trees where you can sit and watch the world go by.

KING HEROD'S WINTER PALACE

King Herod the Great used to rule this region as governor. Even though it was the Roman emperor who was really in power, Herod loved to have an important title and a luxurious lifestyle.

You can see the winter palace he had built in Jericho. Its position well below sea level ensured a warm climate during the winter months even when the rest of Judea was bitterly cold. The palace is still used by government officials.

For a fee, a servant will take you on a tour of the gardens.

MUST SEE!

KING HEROD USED TO LOVE TO COME AND SIT HERE.

JOSHUA ENTERS JERICHO

Jericho has been built and destroyed many times over its long history. One story from the Old Testament of the Bible is of the people of Israel taking the city. Their leader, Joshua, gave orders that he said were from God – to march around the city on each of seven days. On the seventh day, priests blew trumpets, the people shouted… and Jericho's mighty fortifications fell down.

BEST BUY

The story of the walls of Jericho falling down has led to the city becoming a centre for the production of ram's horn trumpets, known as shofars.
They make good souvenirs although producing an appealing sound is not very easy!

JESUS FACT FILE

Jesus and the tax collector

Jesus came through Jericho on his way to Jerusalem. The stories say that a hugely unpopular tax collector named Zacchaeus got pushed to the back of the welcoming crowd. He climbed a tree to see Jesus. Jesus noticed him and asked to stay at his house. After a long conversation with Jesus, Zacchaeus promised to give half his possessions to the poor and to pay back four times what he owed to anyone he had cheated.

People have to pay taxes to the Roman rulers. These silver coins show the Roman emperors Tiberius and Augustus.

Approaching Jerusalem

Bethphage is another traditional village. It is on the road from Bethany to Jerusalem.

There are various different roads that lead to Jerusalem – such as from Bethlehem in the south and Samaria in the north. If you're coming from Jericho, you will pass through wild country, which is a notorious spot for bandits. Try to travel with a large group.

From villages near Jerusalem, you can hire a donkey to go into the city. Locals frequently use donkeys to take their produce to market. Jesus once rode a donkey to Jerusalem from the village of Bethphage and now tourists can take the same route.

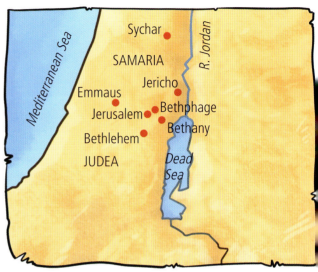

Jerusalem and the surrounding area

KEEP GOING, DONKEY!

TOURIST TIP

If you want to reach Jerusalem by donkey, make sure you take care: many of the roads approaching the city have steep ascents and descents and you could find yourself slipping off.

JESUS FACT FILE

Jesus enters Jerusalem

Jesus caused quite a stir when he rode on a donkey from Bethphage to Jerusalem. The crowds waved palm branches and cheered him as their next king, shouting out, "God bless the king, who comes in the name of the Lord!"

But the religious authorities felt threatened by Jesus and wanted to find a reason to arrest him.

Jerusalem

The ancient city of Jerusalem is one of the most interesting places to visit in all Palestine and not to be missed.

HISTORY

Jerusalem is a walled city set on a hill. It became the capital of the people of Israel, today's Jews, about 1,000 years BC. The people's greatest king, David, captured an existing fort and made it his own. The stories say that his men sprang a surprise attack from inside, having climbed through the shaft which carried water into the citadel from the Gihon Spring outside the city walls.

KING HEZEKIAH

Around 300 years later, a king named Hezekiah took advantage of the same spring to make sure the city had enough water to last a long siege by the Assyrian army.

Nowadays there are tours to see the tunnel that he had cut in order to channel water to a cistern inside the walls.

I CAN'T WAIT TO LOOK AROUND JERUSALEM!

A diagram of Jerusalem, showing the new city walls, added by King Herod Agrippa I, the grandson of King Herod the Great

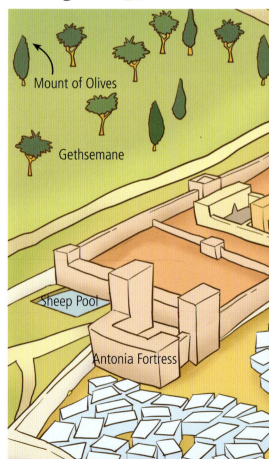

Mount of Olives

Gethsemane

Sheep Pool

Antonia Fortress

TODAY'S SKYLINE

Jerusalem today is the result of building work by the Romans and also by King Herod the Great.

WHAT TO SEE

As you might expect, there is plenty for visitors to see and do. Highlights include:

- the Temple
- the Antonia Fortress
- Herod's palace
- the Mount of Olives.

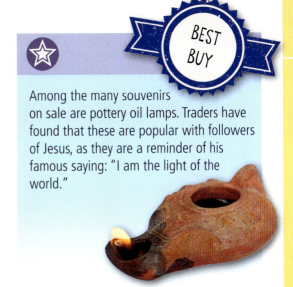

BEST BUY

Among the many souvenirs on sale are pottery oil lamps. Traders have found that these are popular with followers of Jesus, as they are a reminder of his famous saying: "I am the light of the world."

Gihon Spring

Temple

Golgotha

Herod's palace

The Temple

Gleaming white and gold, the Temple in Jerusalem is breathtakingly beautiful and the city's main attraction.

It is a place full of activity – in addition to the priests, temple workers, scribes, teachers, and lawyers who work here, there are many members of the public and tourists who come to worship.

Street traders and shopkeepers outside the Temple precinct ply their wares to passers-by.

This is the third Temple built on this site. Construction of this building was ordered by King Herod the Great and began in 19 BC.

MUST SEE!

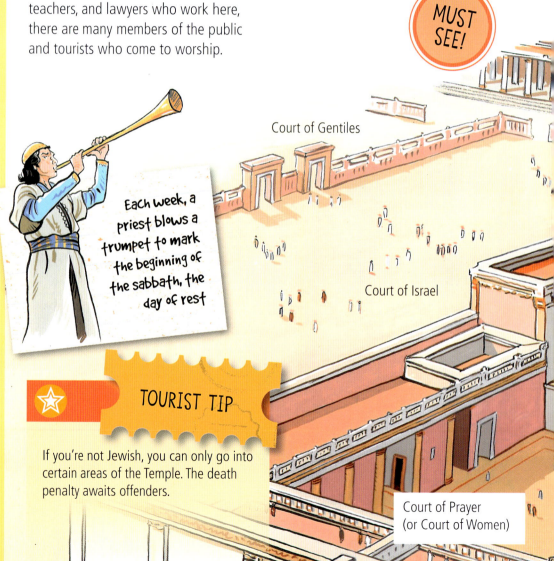

Each week, a priest blows a trumpet to mark the beginning of the sabbath, the day of rest

Court of Gentiles

Court of Israel

TOURIST TIP

If you're not Jewish, you can only go into certain areas of the Temple. The death penalty awaits offenders.

Court of Prayer (or Court of Women)

THE HOLY OF HOLIES

Inside the Temple Sanctuary is the most important place in the Temple, the "Holy of Holies". It is screened off by a large curtain and only the high priest is allowed to enter. Three objects are kept here: the altar of incense, the menorah (the seven-branched lampstand), and the table of showbread.

Scriptures say that God gave Moses stone tablets inscribed with laws called the Ten Commandments. He placed the tablets into the ark of the covenant, but, to this day, no one knows what happened to it.

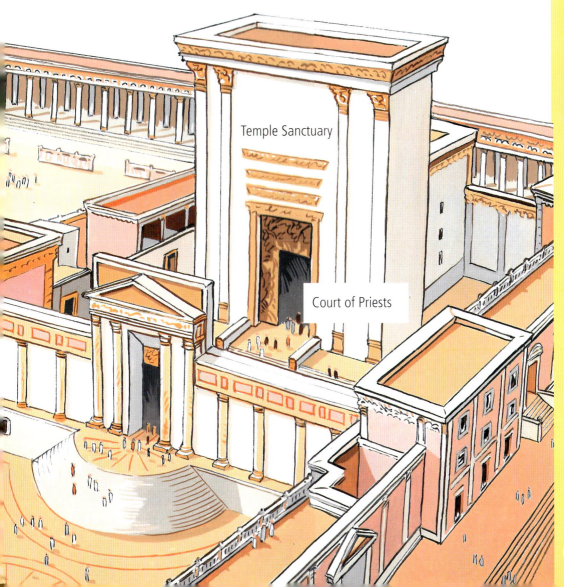

Temple Sanctuary

Court of Priests

The Antonia Fortress and the City Walls

Right next to the Temple in Jerusalem is the Roman fortress, the Antonia. Built by King Herod the Great, the Antonia has spacious accommodation and courtyards for the cohort of soldiers permanently stationed here. There is a tower at each of its corners, enabling the guards to have a good view of the whole Temple area.

Visitors to the city should be aware that tensions between the Jews and their Roman occupiers are running high. At festival times soldiers are stationed along the walls overlooking the Temple compound to watch the people and stop any uprisings.

DEAD MAN'S WALK

There is a road that leads from the Antonia Fortress along narrow streets to one of the gates in the city walls. This is the way that guards take criminals to be executed. You can often see bodies hanging on wooden crosses on the hill outside the city called Calvary, where crucifixions take place.

MUST SEE!

Antonia Fortress

A Roman gaming board carved into a pavement in Jerusalem

CITY WALLS

Since the time of King Herod the Great, the suburbs to the north of Jerusalem have grown considerably. A couple of years before King Herod Agrippa I died in AD 44 he decided to build a new wall to enclose this part of the city.

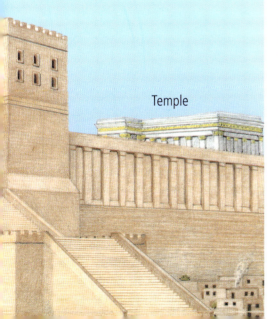

Temple

 JESUS FACT FILE

The way of the cross

Jesus was led by soldiers from the Antonia Fortress along the city streets, through a gate in the walls, and up to Calvary, where he was crucified. Throughout this journey he was forced to carry his own heavy cross.

Jesus is said to have been laid in a stone-cut tomb. Like many other tombs of this kind that can be seen outside the city walls, it had a rolling stone door, which would have been set in a groove.

Resurrection

The story goes that when some of the mourners went back to the tomb a few days after Jesus' death, they found the door open and the body gone.

His followers say that God raised him to life. They claim that Jesus was then with them for forty days, appearing numerous times, before going up to heaven.

Roman soldiers were present at Jesus' death

Festivals

Jerusalem and the Temple area become very lively at festival time. Here are some key festivals. Note that the dates vary from year to year.

PASSOVER (PESACH)

This important spring festival takes place around March. It recalls an event in the history of the people of Israel, when they were slaves in Egypt. God chose a man named Moses to lead them to freedom in a new land where they could make their home.

On the night they were due to leave, the people marked their houses a special way, as instructed by God. Death struck the homes of the Egyptians but "passed over" the homes of Moses' people.

Bitter herbs are part of the Passover meal, to remind Jews of the dark times their ancestors experienced as slaves in Egypt

PENTECOST (SHAVUOT)

This is a festival marking the wheat harvest and comes fifty days after Passover.

SHELTERS (SUKKOT)

After Moses led the people out of Egypt they spent many years in the Sinai wilderness, living as nomads and trusting in God. Ever since, the people have lived in shelters made of branches for a few days each autumn.

LIGHTS (HANUKKAH)

This festival celebrates the bravery of a Jewish freedom fighter named Judas Maccabeus who wanted to remove the statues in the Temple put there by foreign rulers. He had the Temple put to rights and held a celebration. Although there was only enough oil left for one day, the menorah burned for eight days, the time needed to prepare more oil. An eight-day festival was declared to commemorate this miracle, and it is celebrated each December by lighting candles on a nine-branched menorah.

The menorah used for Hanukkah

 ## JESUS FACT FILE

Passover

Jesus came to Jerusalem for Passover when he was a boy, aged twelve. He got lost and was later found in the Temple, talking to the religious leaders.

As an adult, Jesus came to Jerusalem on a donkey at Passover time. When he saw the cheating of the traders and moneychangers within the Temple precinct he was filled with rage and drove out the stallholders. Not long after, he was betrayed and crucified.

Pentecost

After Jesus' death his followers went into hiding. But at Pentecost that year, something happened to make them bold. Some say God's Spirit came upon them. They burst into the streets crowded with pilgrims who had come for the festival and began calling on people to follow Jesus.

Hanukkah

Jesus once came to the Temple in Jerusalem for this festival.

The Mount of Olives

The Mount of Olives is a hill to the east of Jerusalem. It is, as the name hints, covered in olive groves.

It's a nice shady place for a quiet day.

SECRET PASSAGE

The Gihon Spring used to flow into the valley between the Mount of Olives and Jerusalem. It is said that King David's men attacked the hilltop fort by creeping through a cave in the hillside and then climbing up the water shaft that led from the spring into the city (see also page 44). Guides will offer to show you the entrance to the cave, but are unlikely to have reliable information.

The Mount of olives

City Wall

Gethsemane

Gihon Spring

Mount of Olives

UNDER THE STARS

Jerusalem gets a lot of visitors, especially at festival times. For this reason, wild camping is generally permitted on the Mount of Olives.

WHAT A LOVELY PLACE TO CAMP!

JESUS FACT FILE

Jesus is arrested

Jesus and his followers went to the Mount of Olives after sharing the Passover meal together. He had told the others that he would be betrayed by one of them. Only he knew it was Judas Iscariot. After a while they went to Gethsemane nearby, where Jesus prayed, while his close friends slept. It was here that Jesus was arrested. He was put on trial and soon condemned to death.

TOURIST TIP

Remember the basic rules:
* Don't damage the trees.
* Don't light fires and take care with lit lamps.
* Don't make noise after dark.
* Take your rubbish with you.

Day Trip to Bethlehem

From Jerusalem it is just a few kilometres south to Bethlehem. Both King David and Jesus were born here.

The followers of Jesus tell stories of his birth in Bethlehem, and that Jesus' family – Mary and Joseph – could also trace their roots back to David. These stories also say that shepherds on the hillsides at night saw an angel, who told them that Jesus had been born, and that he was going to be a king like David.

I WAS JUST A LAD, BUT I SAW IT ALL!

Inn

Guests

ROOM SHARE

It is said that Jesus was born in a stable and cradled in a manger.

To this day some of the poorer houses are very simply arranged with one lower area for the animals and an upper room for the family. People who live in such houses may offer you the chance to spend a night alongside an ox and an ass, as Mary, Joseph, and Jesus did.

MUST SEE!

Animal stable

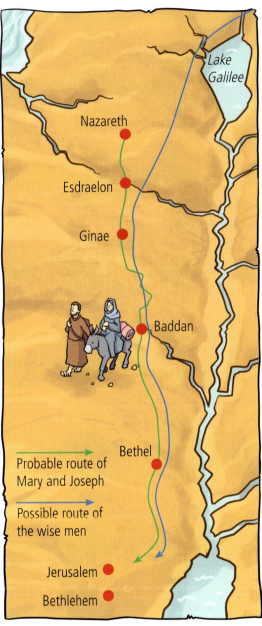

Lake Galilee

Nazareth

Esdraelon

Ginae

Baddan

Bethel

→ Probable route of Mary and Joseph

→ Possible route of the wise men

Jerusalem

Bethlehem

Mary and Joseph travelled from Nazareth to Bethlehem, probably along this route. When Jesus was still very young he was visited by wise men from the East.

Day Trip to Bethany

Bethany is a lovely country village, just outside Jerusalem, and is worth a visit. Home to farmers and craftworkers, it is a busy place with a closely knit community and traditional way of life.

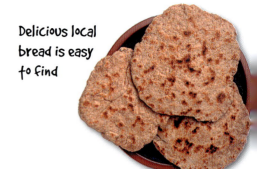

Delicious local bread is easy to find

Bakery

Village well

JESUS FACT FILE

Jesus, Martha, and Mary

The story goes that Jesus visited a house in Bethany where two sisters, named Martha and Mary, lived with their brother Lazarus. Martha was upset because Mary sat listening to Jesus while she did all the work.

Jesus told her that she was worried over so many small things that could wait, but Mary had chosen rightly to listen to him while she could.

Jesus and Lazarus

Locals tell of a miracle that Jesus worked here. One time, Lazarus was seriously ill. Martha and Mary sent a message to Jesus to come but by the time he arrived it was too late: their brother had died and had already been buried in a tomb. But Jesus ordered the stone in front of the tomb to be removed and called, "Lazarus, come out!" Immediately Lazarus walked out, alive. Everyone was amazed.

Tourists can go and visit Lazarus's tomb, which is like a cave built into the rock.

Where Next?

Galilee and the surrounding regions in Palestine are just one holiday destination. Roman rule around the Mediterranean Sea has opened up routes to many places.

Pilgrims from all over the empire were in Jerusalem for Pentecost when the followers of Jesus began their preaching.

Since then, believers have begun making journeys around the empire spreading the news.

⭐ JESUS FACT FILE

The day of Pentecost

It is said that when Jesus' followers preached on the day of Pentecost, pilgrims heard them speaking in their own local languages.

Rome

SICILY

MALTA

Temple at Ephesus

Roman theatre, Philippi

LET'S START PLANNING OUR NEXT TRIP!

Philippi

essalonica

Ephesus

Colossae

Antioch

Athens

Corinth

CYPRUS

CRETE

Damascus

Mediterranean Sea

Caesarea

Jerusalem

Index

ID Card

NAME _____

AGE _____

ROMAN CITIZEN

Yes ☐

No ☐

stick picture here

PROFESSION _____

I WONDER HOW MUCH MONEY WE'LL NEED?

CURRENCY

Use our handy guide to make sure you know which coins you are going to need when you travel.

New Testament

Roman	Greek	Jewish
	Lepton (bronze) (plural, lepta)	
Quadrans (= 2 lepta)		
As (= 4 quadrans)		
Denarius (= 16 as)	Drachma (silver)	
	Di-drachma (= 2 drachmae)	(Used as a half-shekel)
	Stater (silver) (= 4 drachmae)	Shekel
Aureus (gold) (= 25 denarii)		
100 denarii =	Mina =	30 shekels
240 aurei =	Talent (= 60 minas)	

To explore more about Bible times, check out these other books from Lion Children's...

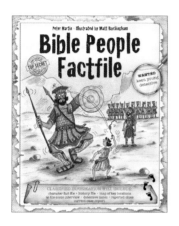

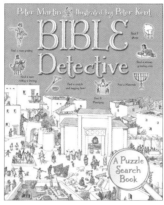

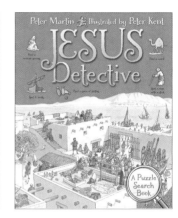

Bible People Fact File

Wanted: keen young detective! Examine the evidence, character files, locations, interviews with witnesses, sift through the clues and decide for yourself who are the heroes, who are the villains, and what REALLY happened...

Jesus Detective/Bible Detective

Young detectives will never tire of this picture-search puzzle book. Readers can pore over cleverly illustrated scenes of Bible events to find the answers to the questions posed on each page. Some puzzles involve looking for details of everyday life, others highlight things that happened in the Bible stories – offering hours of fun to readers as they search for the answers. Warning: may be addictive!

LION
CHILDREN'S